Smart Cities

Integrating Sustainable Design and Eco-Friendly Practices into Urban Environment

Table of Contents

Chapter 1. Introduction

As urban populations continue to burgeer, the call to redefine and reengineer our cities has become more pressing than ever. Welcome to our Special Report titled "Smart Cities: Integrating Sustainable Design and Eco-Friendly Practices into Urban Environment". It's an exploration of how modern technology, innovative thinking, and responsible practices are acting in unison to craft the metropolises of the future. We traverse the globe analyzing groundbreaking developments, from photovoltaic pathways in Amsterdam to eco-cities in China, and dive deep into smart solutions to urban densification issues. Welcome to a journey that is both enthusiastic and enlightening, underscored by an enduring respect for our planet. Reading this report won't just keep you informed—it will inspire you to participate in this transformative era of sustainable urban living. This is no mere dream of a utopian future; it's a well-researched, practical guide catering to city developers, planners, environmentalists, technocrats, and you. Dive in to discover how you can contribute to making our cities smarter, greener, and more sustainable places for us all. Empower yourself to be part of this exciting intelligent urban revolution!

Chapter 2. Defining Smart Cities: An Introduction

A smart city, at its most basic definition, is an urban locale that utilizes various forms of digital technology to enhance the lives of the citizens that inhabit it. Technological innovations, primarily led by information technology services, are used to increase efficiency, reduce wastage, increase sustainability, and improve quality of life. As our urban environments continue to burgeon, the necessity for such smart, integrated approaches is becoming an urgent priority.

2.1. The Framework of a Smart City

Understanding the intricacies of a smart city begins with a look at its fundamental framework. A smart city fundamentally integrates physical, information and human systems in a built environment to fuel sustainable economic growth and enhance the quality of life for its citizens. This is achieved through the provision of services such as transport, electricity, security and emergency services, recycling, and education, amongst others.

Information and Communication Technology (ICT), and more importantly the Internet of Things (IoT), serve as the central nervous system of the smart city. By interconnecting various digital devices and platforms, communication is enabled to flow seamlessly, ensuring city systems work together efficiently.

Sensors are a key component of the ICT, gathering data from everywhere in the city. This data can be about anything from traffic levels, air quality, electricity usage, or waste. This data is then processed and utilized in real-time to create instant solutions to urban problems.

2.2. Sustainable Practices and Eco-friendliness

One of the key factors that differentiates a smart city from a regular one is its focus on sustainability and eco-friendly practices. Modern urban landscapes are too often characterized by pollution, waste, and a lack of green space, factors that significantly diminish the quality of life for residents.

Smart city design aims to integrate nature back into the urban landscape, creating green spaces that allow residents to connect with their natural environment. Parks, green roofs, and community gardens can play a key role in this effort, while also helping to manage stormwater runoff and reduce heat island effects in summer.

In addition, smart cities aspire to reduce waste, conserve water, and minimize energy usage. Waste diversion programs, water recycling initiatives, and energy-efficient buildings and infrastructure are all common features in a smart city.

On an even deeper level, smart cities are aiming to become carbon neutral or carbon negative. This involves not just reducing their own emissions, but investing in renewable energy projects and carbon offsetting initiatives.

2.3. Urban Densification

Another issue that smart city design seeks to tackle is urban densification. As the global population continues to increase, cities are becoming more and more crowded. This results in a variety of problems, including housing shortages, increased energy consumption, greater pollution, and overwhelmed infrastructure.

Smart urban planning aims to create high-density, mixed-use

developments that are walkable, bike-able, and easily accessible by public transport. Good urban planning also means balancing residential needs with commercial and industrial needs, and making sure that all communities have access to essential services.

Smart building technologies play a key role in managing urban densification. These technologies can help increase energy efficiency, reduce water waste, and improve the overall comfort and convenience of urban living.

2.4. Challenges and Opportunities

Despite the many benefits that smart cities offer, they also face a variety of challenges. Firstly, building a smart city from the ground up is a significant undertaking that requires substantial financial investment. Secondly, the technology required to run a smart city is complex and rapidly evolving, requiring constant updating and adaptation.

Additionally, as with all digitally integrated networks, security is a major concern. The vast amounts of data being collected and processed on a daily basis presents a tempting target for hackers, and protecting that data is a significant challenge.

Despite these challenges, the potential benefits of smart cities far outweigh the difficulties. The opportunity to create sustainable, livable cities that are resilient in the face of climate change and other challenges is too great to ignore.

As our world continues to urbanize, the concept of smart cities provides a viable path forward. When powered by the right technology and steered by visionary leadership, these cities can play a crucial role in ushering in a more sustainable, equitable, and habitable future for all.

In the next chapters, we will delve deeper into the various aspects that make a city "smart", exploring case studies, successes, and lessons learned around the world, and gleaning insights that might be applied to future urban developments. From Amsterdam to Shanghai, you'll discover the inspiring stories of cities leading the way in the smart city revolution and gain invaluable perspectives on how you, too, can contribute to the sustainability of your own urban environment.

Chapter 3. The Intersection of Technological Innovation and Urban Planning

Cities are the epicenters of human activity, with more than half of the world's population expected to live in urban areas by mid-century. As these cities grow and evolve, urban planners and technologists are faced with a compelling challenge and opportunity: How do we use technological innovation to create livable, sustainable, and efficient urban environments? This challenge lies at the heart of understanding and improving the intersection of technological innovation and urban planning.

3.1. The Role of Technology in Urban Planning

Understanding the role of technology in urban planning starts with acknowledging that the process of planning and development has largely remained the same over the past century. However, the table is turning. The emergence of hyper-connectivity, Internet of Things (IoT), Artificial Intelligence (AI), and data analytics are opening new avenues for creating more responsive and dynamic urban spaces.

Hyper-connectivity and IoT enable city infrastructures and devices to be interconnected, enabling real-time monitoring and improvement of city operations. AI takes it a step further by providing predictive capabilities, as it can analyze patterns and predict future outcomes. This feature can impact everything, from traffic management to resource allocation and disaster response.

Data is an indispensable asset in smart urban planning. The use of big data helps planners understand city dynamics, track resource consumption, monitor urban growth and decline, and react proactively to urban issues. Data collection from various sources - social media, satellite imagery, mobile devices, IoT sensors, and more - provide city planners with accurate and timely information with which to make decisions.

3.2. Smarter Urban Spaces

One of the main benefits of integrating technology into urban planning is the creation of smarter urban spaces. For instance, digitally connected public transportation systems can help streamline commutes, reduce traffic congestion and decrease carbon emissions.

Smart lighting systems use sensors and IoT technology to control municipal lighting based on natural light levels, pedestrian and vehicular traffic. This mechanism not only enhances public safety but also minimizes energy consumption. From Amsterdam's connected streetlight network to Los Angeles' adaptive lighting initiative, cities worldwide are leveraging smart lighting systems to contribute to energy efficiency.

Furthermore, smart waste management models such as sensor-equipped bins help manage solid waste more efficiently, providing real-time data on waste levels. Information on waste generation and management aids city planners in developing programs that reduce landfill waste and promote recycling and composting.

3.3. Technolgy and The Future of City Planning

Though technology offers numerous advantages, it is crucial to analyze potential drawbacks. Technological interventions run the risk of exacerbating socio-economic disparities if not accessible to all.

Therefore, while considering technology's role in urban planning, equitable access to resources and opportunities must be prioritized.

Futuristic city planning also involves integrating urban spaces with vertical greenery, solar power installations and buildings with automated energy-saving systems. Such "eco-friendly smart buildings" are self-sustaining entities and can greatly contribute to carbon neutrality in dense urban environments.

Looking ahead, cities of the future are likely to be test-beds for autonomous transportation, including self-driving cars, drones, and other unmanned vehicles. As autonomous technology grows more mature and widespread, city planners will need to consider how these technologies can be safely and efficiently integrated into an increasingly complex urban landscape.

Another crucial aspect is cybersecurity. As city infrastructure gets more digital and interconnected, protecting these systems from cyber-attacks becomes paramount. Consequently, cybersecurity will, and must, play a leading role in urban planning strategies of the future.

3.4. Encouraging Innovative City Design

The intersection of technology and urban planning is about more than just incorporating new technologies into city services. It entails a change in our approach to city planning itself, and a shift towards encouraging innovative thinking when it comes to city design.

Cities like Copenhagen, Stockholm, and Singapore are leaders in adopting smart solutions. Their success stories can serve as blueprints for future city planners. These cities have shown that the path to intelligent urban living is through a combination of bold innovation, thoughtful design and planning, data utilization, and collaborative effort among stakeholders.

Initiatives such as 'living labs' encourage sustainable urban planning and smart city solutions. These platforms bring together researchers, municipal authorities, businesses, and citizens to co-create innovative solutions.

The intersection of technology and urban planning is not a new concept, but it is one that is continually evolving. As technology progresses, so do our cities, and the way we envision, design, and interact with them. However, the ultimate goal remains unchanging: to create urban spaces that are sustainable, efficient, and comfortable for all who inhabit them.

With thoughtful design, strategic planning, and considered technology integration, our cities have the potential to be not just places of residence but catalysts for sustainable living and societal growth. The journey is one of discovery and understanding, of learning from past experiences, and envisioning a future where urban living is not just a necessity but a part of an integrated, sustainable ecosystem. And it all starts at the intersection of technological innovation and urban planning.

Chapter 4. Globetrotting: Case Studies of Sustainable Cities Worldwide

Our exploration commences with a journey that transverses the globe to scrutinize the sustainable initiatives established in diverse cities. From extensive renewable energy projects to ensuring reliable and clean public transportation, these cities are successfully showcasing the pathway to a sustainable future.

4.1. Cycling to the Future: Amsterdam, The Netherlands

Amsterdam, the capital city of The Netherlands, has been renowned for its bicycling culture, wherein over 900,000 bicycles are estimated to be in the city—more than the population itself. The city has transformed itself into a bicycle paradise, reducing its carbon footprint and promoting a healthier lifestyle among its inhabitants.

Moreover, to support its massive biking culture, Amsterdam has integrated smart technology with street paving to push the boundaries of sustainability. Solaroad, a collaboration between the local government and several private entities, developed a prototype of a road that doubles as a solar panel. The 70-meter pathway, made of concrete modules embedded with solar cells and covered with a translucent layer of tempered glass, can generate enough electricity to power three households.

Amsterdam's application of integrated renewable energy efforts to an already existing sustainable mode of transportation not only redefines innovative thinking but also serves as a testament to the city's unwavering commitment to sustainability.

4.2. The Garden City: Singapore

In South-East Asia, the island city of Singapore demonstrates how a small land area doesn't necessarily present a limitation when balanced harmoniously with sustainable urban design and nature. Known as a "Garden City," Singapore is a model for urban green spaces.

Singapore's smart and sustainable design extends beyond remarkable parks and trees. An excellent example is the integration of nature with architecture in building designs such as the "tree-like" columns at the National Gallery and the solar-powered "supertrees" at Gardens by the Bay. Furthermore, these structures not only enhance city aesthetics but also function to the city's ecological advantage by contributing to its cooling effect, improving air quality, and upkeeping biodiversity.

With around 80 percent of its residents living in public housing, Singapore has also ventured into sustainable public housing. West Terra @ Bukit Batok, a housing project, takes the spotlight with its significant green initiatives. The development utilizes smart technology, such as energy-saving LED lights in communal areas and rainwater harvesting systems for non-potable water usage.

4.3. The Eco-Cities of China: Tianjin Eco-City

Tianjin Eco-City was designed with a primary vision of achieving harmony with nature, economic development, and a sustainable socioeconomic environment.

The city runs on a multi-layered transportation network featuring a Light Rail Transit system and electronic personal rapid transit (PRT). The PRT system, similar to a taxi but automatic and no carbon emissions, serves the residents as a transit service for the less densely populated areas.

Moreover, Tianjin Eco-City emphasizes energy efficiency, with 20% of its energy sourced from renewable energies like solar and wind power. Waste management is another field where the city has made significant strides. It treats and reuses about 60% of its sewage, transforming waste into a resource.

4.4. Embracing Sustainability: Copenhagen, Denmark

Recognized many times over as a leader in sustainability, the City of Copenhagen embodies a sophisticated blend of smart technology, renewable energy, and eco-friendly practices in its pursuit of becoming carbon neutral by 2025.

The city's portfolio of sustainable and renewable energy solutions is impressive. Among them stands the city's extensive bicycle network, which boasts over 450 kilometers of bike lanes and seeing bike usage exceeding car usage.

Copenhagen is also home to one of the world's most significant offshore wind farm developments—the Middelgrunden wind farm. Wind power now satisfies more than half of the city's electricity needs.

4.5. The Green Tech City: Stockholm, Sweden

Named as the first-ever European Green Capital, Stockholm embodies a city that has built sustainability into its core. Implementing significant measures to reduce fossil fuel usage, Stockholm aims to be entirely fossil-fuel-free by 2040.

The Hammarby Sjöstad district showcases Stockholm's commitment to sustainability, featuring eco-friendly buildings, waste-to-energy recycling, and an advanced public transportation system.

Stockholm's bold and conscious decision to integrate sustainable design and renewable energy into city planning defines it as one of the pioneers in the smart and green city movement.

Across the globe, cities are redesigning themselves to adapt and evolve into smart and sustainable entities. These pioneering locations demonstrate possibilities while simultaneously serving as schematics for what might be achievable on a much larger scale. As we continue to redefine our urban landscapes in this era of rapid urbanization, these examples provide valuable insights into our path of creating cities that prioritize sustainability.

Chapter 5. The Role of AI and IoT in Creating Eco-Friendly Urban Spaces

Artificial Intelligence (AI) and the Internet of Things (IoT) are making substantial contributions in shaping eco-friendly urban spaces as they breed a new era of eco-efficient solutions, from scaling renewable energy to managing waste optimally.

5.1. AI, IoT, and the Idea of Smart Cities

A smart city is inherently one that leverages technology, specifically AI and IoT, to deal with urban challenges while reducing environmental impact. Each device, be it a traffic light or a waste bin, becomes an important node of the IoT network. The city turns into an intricate system that can self-regulate the flow of traffic, consumption of energy, and emission of pollutants in real-time. AI comes in to process and analyse the colossal amount of data provided by these devices, thereby enabling informed, environment-friendly decisions.

5.2. Powering Green Energies

The digitization of the power grid has opened new ways for optimizing energy consumption and facilitating the integration of renewable energies. AI-driven approaches allow the prediction of patterns namely, dynamic grid management, anticipating energy demand, and production. These predictive models use data from smart meters, weather forecasts, and user habits for a more sustained approach to energy use.

Moreover, AI is paralled with IoT to balance the supply and demand of energy in a decentralized and eco-friendly manner. When excess energy is produced, smart grids equipped with AI redirect it to where it's needed or store it for future use instead of wasting it.

5.3. Waste Management and Recycling

In urban areas, waste management is a daunting task with enormous environmental implications. IoT enabled waste management systems are now ensuring waste collection, disposal, and recycling processes become smarter and more efficient. Sensors fitted in waste bins transmit data about how full they are, allowing for pickup route optimization and a reduction in needless trips.

AI, in turn, has a transformational effect on waste sorting and recycling. Sophisticated AI technology can segregate waste items for recycling with precision, reducing human labor while diverting a higher amount of waste from landfills.

5.4. Smart Buildings: Efficiency through Automation

Smart buildings represent another aspect in which AI and IoT are making significant strides towards sustainability. IoT sensors can monitor a vast array of factors in a building such as temperature, light, and occupancy. This data, processed using AI, can contribute to real-time, dynamic adjustment of the building's systems to enhance energy efficiency.

Air conditioning systems can adapt according to the number of people in the room and lighting systems can adjust to natural light availability. These are but a few of the numerous ways in which smart buildings are fostering a reduction in energy consumption and greenhouse gas emissions.

5.5. Traffic and Transport Systems

Traffic congestion is a critical problem in urban cities that not only affects productivity but also contributes significantly to air pollution. AI and IoT are being employed to alleviate this issue. The data provided by IoT enabled traffic systems like smart signals, GPS enabled vehicles, and cameras can be analyzed using AI.

This helps predict traffic hotspots, devising optimal traffic flow strategies, and providing real-time rerouting options for drivers. Furthermore, it aids in developing efficient public transportation schedules that can decrease the number of vehicles on the road.

Modern cities must consider environmental sustainability alongside urban growth. Fortunately, the synergy of AI and IoT has paved the way for a genuinely symbiotic relationship between urbanization and eco-consciousness. They not only provide solutions for present environmental issues but also open avenues for sustainable innovation, proving to be the cornerstone of futuristic smart cities.

Though it brings new challenges in terms of data privacy and technology regulation, the promise outweighs these concerns. As we step ahead to build smart, eco-friendly cities, it is critical to understand the role of AI and IoT and ensure their responsible adoption.

This detailed examination serves not only city planners and environmentalists but also every individual keen on understanding how smart cities will influence their lives – and how they, in turn, can participate in this exciting phase of urban evolution.

Through fostering technology-aware, environmentally conscious citizenry, we can ensure the desired synergy of urban development and environmental sustainability turns from a mere possibility into reality.

Chapter 6. Blueprint for the Future: Sustainable Residential and Commercial Designs

There's a rising urgency to address the impact of urbanization on our environment. And it is within this context that architects, designers, urban planners, and technologists across the globe are envisioning and manifesting a new reality in sustainable residential and commercial designs.

6.1. The Core of Sustainable Design

At the heart of sustainable design lies the aspiration to lessen the adverse effects of building constructions on human health and our environment. This is achieved by efficiently using energy, water, and other resources, protecting occupant wellbeing, and reducing waste, pollution, and environmental degradation. Throughout is weaved the practice of resilience, facilitating building designs to weather change, and not just persist, but thrive under evolving conditions.

A stapling feature of sustainable design is passive solar design. It includes orienting buildings to the sun, selecting insulative materials, installing efficient windows, and adopting devices such as solar panels and solar water heaters. This orientation to natural cycles doesn't merely save energy but leads to interior spaces that are naturally more comfortable and pleasurable to inhabit.

The integration of vegetation, whether as simple green roofs or complex vertical gardens, is another unmistakable feature. Greenery absorbs carbon dioxide and releases oxygen improving air quality, while also providing shade, reducing stormwater runoff, and enhancing biodiversity.

6.2. Innovative Residential Designs

The path to sustainable residential design is broad and varied, interlacing different sectors and drawing respective expertise.

Net-zero-energy homes are becoming increasingly prevalent. These highly energy-efficient homes generate their own energy locally through renewable sources like solar, wind, or ground-source heat pumps, producing as much or even more energy as they consume.

An excellent example of this is the Heliotrope House in Germany. Rotating 180 degrees to follow the sun, it uses a combination of passive solar design, a thermal heat sink, solar panels, and triple pane glass to achieve near-zero energy consumption.

Yet sustainability isn't merely about energy efficiency. It's about creating houses that are healthy to live in and are constructed from eco-friendly materials. One such remarkable project is the Grow Community on Bainbridge Island in the United States, where homes are built using less toxic materials, promoting superior indoor air quality.

6.3. Green Commercial Buildings

As sustainable commercial buildings continue to rise in popularity, they not only provide a healthier work environment but also showcase a commitment to sustainable practices.

One shining example is the Bullitt Center in Seattle, USA, often dubbed the 'greenest commercial building in the world'. This six-story building is a zero-energy build, capturing rainwater, composting waste, and applying sustainable wood throughout.

In Japan, the ACROS Fukuoka building has achieved a fantastic synthesis of commercial development and green design. It transforms what would have been a 14-story wall of glass into a lush, cascading mountain of plant life.

6.4. Building Materials and Construction

The raw materials that constitute our buildings are as significant as the architecture. So, innovations in materials and construction methods, all underpinned by cutting-edge research, are adding another tier of sustainability.

Straw bales, for example, have made a comeback as an affordable, locally-sourced, highly-insulative, and carbon-neutral building material. Similarly, rammed earth — a technology as old as human civilization itself, is seeing a resurgence, both in low-rise urban dwellings and high-end real estate.

Hempcrete, made from the inner woody core of the hemp plant mixed with a lime-based binder, is another building material that deserves mention. It's not just carbon-neutral but carbon-negative, absorbing more carbon over its lifecycle than is emitted in its production.

6.5. Forward, Towards Recovery

The road to recovery lies in redesigning our cities, homes, and workspaces to be more in tune with the planet and its resources. Whether it's a complete rebuilding or ecological retrofitting, embracing sustainable residential and commercial designs will pave the path to a rejuvenated future.

Sustainability is no longer a fringe element of architecture; it is being woven into its DNA. While we still have a long way to go, each stride takes us closer to a future where our cities and buildings are not just spires of human civilization but testaments to our ability to coexist with nature.

We end with the words of architect William McDonough, inventor of the Cradle to Cradle philosophy, who said, "Design is the first signal of human intention." Let our intention, through our building designs, be to protect and nourish the Earth and its inhabitants. This blueprint for a sustainable future can only be achieved through our collective, persistent effort and an unwavering commitment to the planet we call home.

Chapter 7. Solar Cities and Beyond: The Power of Renewable Energy in Urban Development

It's dawn in a city of the future. The sleepless metropolis hums with energy, but unlike the cities of yesteryears, no plumes of smoke rise to stain the morning sky. Instead, the rising sun meets a stunning array of solar panels glistening on rooftops, facades, and even streets, all silently feeding the urban electricity grid with clean, renewable energy. From heating water to powering transportation, solar energy is ushering in a new era, transforming cities into self-sustaining ecosystems.

7.1. Solar Power: A Brief Overview

Sunlight is a renewable energy source that's freely available, abundant, and non-polluting. By leveraging Photovoltaics (PV) and Concentrated Solar Power (CSP), cities can convert sunlight into electricity, a process devoid of any greenhouse gas emission. Photovoltaics directly convert light into electricity using semiconductor materials. They're commonly seen in solar panels installed on rooftops, parking meters, autonomous street lights, and other urban structures. Conversely, CSP generates electricity by focusing a large area of sunlight into a small beam, which is used to produce steam that drives a generator.

7.2. Turning Buildings into Power Stations

The potential of integrating solar-powered technologies in city buildings is vast. Innovations such as solar windows and solar facades not only minimize energy consumption but also generate electricity actively. Solar windows—which bear transparent solar cells—permit visual connection with the outdoor environment while producing electricity. Similarly, BIPV(Building-Integrated Photovoltaics) products like solar facades generate electricity while replacing conventional building materials. Therefore, buildings of the future can be net energy producers rather than consumers.

7.3. The Roadways of the Future

The concept of Solar Roadways—an ambitious project that originated in the U.S.—aims to replace standard asphalt surfaces with robust, solar energy-harvesting panels capable of withstanding the heaviest of trucks. These smart roads could generate enough electricity to power nearby homes and buildings, saving significant amounts of conventional energy.

7.4. Solar-Powered Transportation

Transportation systems powered by solar energy are increasingly becoming a reality. Solar electric vehicles, solar-powered charging stations, and even solar-powered public transportation are all promising developments. The transition to solar can significantly reduce greenhouse gas emissions, air pollution, and reliance on fossil fuel resources. From solar-powered buses in Australia to solar-powered rickshaws in India, the movement towards clean energy transportation is an international one, with significant potential to reduce the carbon footprint of cities worldwide.

7.5. Challenges and Potential Solutions

Despite the compelling benefits of solar energy, several challenges exist. Primary among them are the issues of intermittency, scalability, and the high initial cost of solar technologies. Energy storage systems, such as batteries and thermal storage, could address intermittency problems and store excess energy produced during midday for use after sundown. Innovative solar tech and economies of scale are also expected to bring down the costs of solar energy.

7.6. Real-world Examples of Solar Cities

Many pioneering cities worldwide are hard at work transitioning away from fossil fuels and toward solar power. California's Lancaster city aims to become the first U.S. city to produce more electricity from solar than it uses. Entirely solar-powered cities like Masdar City in the UAE and Tianjin Eco-city in China are pushing the boundaries of sustainability, showing the world that it's possible to create cities that coexist harmoniously with the environment.

In conclusion, the future of urban development depends significantly on how effectively we incorporate renewable energy sources into our cities' DNA. From building-integrated photovoltaics to solar-powered transportation, the transition to a cleaner and more sustainable economy isn't a pipedream any longer, but a real, achievable goal. Harnessing solar power for citywide use represents a significant step towards realizing this goal. With planning, innovation, and collaboration, we can create solar-powered cities that are not only sustainable, but self-sustainable, reducing our environmental footprint while improving quality of urban life.

Chapter 8. Public Transportation: The Road to Reduced Carbon Emissions

Several advances in public transportation capabilities have brought cities tantalizingly close to an era of significantly reduced carbon emissions, augmenting the broader effort to combat climate change. This becomes more critical as sprawling urban populations contribute to higher carbon emissions because of their dependence on fossil fuel-driven automobiles for commuting. For instance, the transportation sector constituted roughly 29% of total US greenhouse gas emissions in 2019—higher than that from any other economic sector. By transitioning to more resource-efficient public transport systems, cities stand a chance to significantly decrease their carbon footprint, thereby propelling urban society toward a more sustainable future.

8.1. The Green Potential of Public Transport

Mass transit systems such as city buses, trams, commuter trains, and metros enable a large number of people to travel simultaneously. Therefore, they use less energy and emit fewer pollutants per passenger than private cars. In fact, if cities can encourage their population to rely more on public transportation, the number of vehicles on the road would decrease, leading to reduced traffic congestion, lowered noise levels, and minimized air pollution.

For context, a full double-decker bus can take up to 75 cars off the road, and one full train can replace over 1,000 cars. Such reductions equate to saving thousands, if not millions, of tons of greenhouse gases that would otherwise be emitted by those cars. Furthermore, public transport networks generally run on fixed routes and schedules, creating a predictable environmental impact that can be more easily quantified, managed, and reduced.

According to a report by the American Public Transportation Association, public transportation in the United States reduces CO_2 emissions by 37 million metric tons annually. This is equivalent to the combined yearly energy usage of about 4.9 million American homes. Undeniably, integrating more efficient, greener public transport systems will constitute a significant stride forward in the global effort to combat climate change.

8.2. The Rise of Electric Buses

Innovative thinking around sustainable public transportation has led to the development of electric buses, revolutionizing urban transit. Unlike their counterparts running on diesel or gasoline, electric buses produce zero tailpipe emissions, significantly contributing to improved air quality. Add to this the potential for these buses to be powered by renewable energy, and you have a viable, green solution to the carbon emissions problem.

China, the world's largest emitter of carbon dioxide, has been particularly progressive in this regard: Shenzhen, a city in southeastern China, was the first to electrify its entire fleet of 16,000 buses in 2018. This effort effectively reduces Shenzhen's carbon emissions by approximately 1.35 million metric tons annually. As other cities worldwide follow this trend, the global shift towards electric buses promises to substantially curb urban carbon emissions.

8.3. The Role of Hybrid Trains

Train travel already has a much smaller carbon footprint compared to cars or planes. However, railways are continually seeking innovative ways to further minimise their environmental impact.

Enter hybrid trains, a promising, eco-friendly alternative for urban and intercity commuting.

These trains work similarly to hybrid cars, having both a conventional internal combustion engine and an electric motor. They can run entirely on electricity when conditions allow, such as when they're inside urban areas or during periods of low demand. When the train stops, the diesel engine can be turned off while the electric motor provides power, leading to substantial energy savings and emission cuts while idling.

The UK was the first to introduce hybrid trains commercially in 2007, and they continue to operate in various parts of the world. Japan is another forerunner in this area, with several hybrid trains operating nationwide. A continued emphasis on the development and expansion of hybrid trains will be a crucial factor in reducing the carbon emissions generated by railway transit.

8.4. Green Metros for Sustainable Commuting

Metros or subways are perhaps the epitome of mass transit in densely populated cities. They boast higher energy efficiency than common road surface transportation modes, mainly due to their electric operation and the large number of passengers they can transport simultaneously.

Today, modern technologies are being deployed to make these metro systems even more sustainable. One such innovation is regenerative braking, which allows the energy released during braking to be captured and returned to the system's power grid, reducing overall energy consumption. Some metro systems also operate on renewable energy, showing the potential to run completely emissions-free.

In Stockholm, the subway extends outside the city to encourage commuting rather than car use. Remarkably, the entire Stockholm metro system operates on electricity, 100% of which comes from renewable sources. Such initiatives set a standard for other urban aggregations to follow when striving for sustainable public transport.

8.5. Conclusion

The road to reduced carbon emissions runs through the heart of the public transportation sector. By transforming conventional mass transit systems into greener, more energy-efficient networks, we can make significant strides towards our sustainability goals. Electric buses, hybrid trains, and green metros are tangible solutions to the carbon emission challenge, and their wider adoption can propel urban society into the future—one where cleaner air, healthier populations, and more liveable cities are a reality, not just a dream.

Over the years, public transportation has gone beyond being a mere means of mobility—into a tool for environmental stewardship. By choosing to commute via public transport, each one of us can actively contribute to curbing carbon emissions. This requires pushing for policies that prioritize public transit's development, advocating for progressive measures in this sector, and embracing these changes at an individual level.

The potential for improvement is significant, and the opportunity for change is vast. In the end, it is not just public transportation riding on this journey—it's the future of our urban environments, the quality of our life, and the health of our planet.

Chapter 9. The Economics of Building Smart Cities: Benefits and Challenges

In today's epoch, the need for novel, sustainable, and progressively efficient societies powered by technology does not only offer a realm of compelling possibilities but presents us with vast challenges that need to be proficiently navigated. The aim of this chapter is to delve into economics underpinning the increasingly dynamic sphere of 'smart cities', boosting a profound understanding of the potential benefits, obstacles, and impacts at an economic level.

9.1. The Economic Imperative of Smart Cities

The fundamental reasoning being the economic imperative of smart cities is intertwined with urban growth, increasing connectivity, and the surge of big data. As per the United Nations, approximately 68% of the world's populace is expected to settle in urban precincts by 2050. This ongoing explosion of urban populations exerts immense pressure on city infrastructures, driving the urgency for more efficient, sustainable, and smart solutions.

From an economic viewpoint, smart cities can unveil substantial benefits. Integrated technology systems enhance the efficiency and efficacy of urban services such as transportation, healthcare, and utilities, leading to cost reductions in the long run. Advanced technologies like the IoT (Internet of Things), AI (Artificial Intelligence), and 5G can help cities move towards predictive rather than reactive models, facilitating better resource allocation. Moreover, smart cities can generate new employment avenues and spur economic growth through innovation and improved quality of life.

9.2. The Proposition of Return on Investment

While looking at the economic benefits of constructing smart cities, one of the crucial aspects to contemplate is the return on investment (ROI). Unlike traditional infrastructure projects, the ROI for smart city initiatives can be considerably more challenging to quantify. This is because benefits frequently manifest as intangible enhancements in citizen's quality of life or long-term efficiencies rather than immediate monetary returns.

However, several models can be employed to better comprehend the potential ROI for smart city transformations. For example, quantifying the time saved from improved public transportation, or calculating the reduced healthcare costs due to better air quality. Hence, when estimating the ROI, it is vital to consider both tangible and intangible returns.

9.3. The Cost of Building Smart Cities

Just as there are potential rewards, the construction of smart cities also involves considerable costs. Incorporating smart technologies into urban infrastructure requires substantial upfront investment. Additionally, the ongoing expenses associated with maintenance, updates, and security measures can be significant.

Cities must also shoulder the costs and challenges of managing and analyzing the enormous volumes of data generated by smart city technologies. With enormous data comes the need for robust data analytics capabilities, requisite storage infrastructure, and cybersecurity measures.

Moreover, there are non-monetary costs to consider. Some citizens may find the increased surveillance associated with smart technologies intrusive, potentially leading to social costs. Additionally, the emphasis on technological solutions could risk deepening digital divide issues within communities.

9.4. Funding and Financing Smart Cities

Where does the capital for adopting these smart technologies come from? Generally, it's a blend of public and private investments. Local authorities might obtain funds from national government initiatives focused on propelling smart city schemes, or international bodies offering grants for such projects.

However, such funding is often insufficient for the substantial investments commonly needed. This drives the necessity for private sector involvement. Public-Private Partnerships (PPPs) are progressively becoming a popular model as they allow risks and rewards to be shared. Private companies can offer the required technical expertise and additional capital, while governments can supply the regulatory support to facilitate such ventures.

Venture capital and angel investors are also increasingly drawn to the potential lucrative benefits of smart cities. Though, with this private investment comes the issue of ensuring the benefits of smart city technologies are widely accessible and do not contribute to growing inequalities in cities.

9.5. Economic Impact of Growing Inequalities

The flip side of the smart city narrative is a widening concern over the risk of increasing inequalities. While the proliferation of advanced technologies is hailed as a landmark development in city planning, it inadvertently runs the risk of creating a deeper chasm between the digital 'haves' and 'have-nots'. To ensure that the benefits of smart cities are truly inclusive, policymakers will need to dedicate substantial resources to close the digital divide.

To summarize, while the potential benefits of smart cities are extensive, so too are the challenges. Understanding the economics of building smart cities is complex and requires considering a broad range of costs, funding sources, and potential impacts. As such, the transition to smarter cities presents not just exciting technological opportunities but important economic and societal questions that warrant careful consideration.

Chapter 10. Engaging Communities in Sustainable City Development

In an era of rapid urban growth, the engagement of local communities in sustainable city development is crucial. Their active participation is a prerequisite for the successful transformation into smart, green, and sustainable metropolises. This engagement happens at multiple levels, encompassing public consultation in planning, citizen involvement in implementation, and community feedback in monitoring and review processes.

10.1. The Importance of Community Involvement

Cities can only be sustainable when they work in harmony with the needs, values, and aspirations of their citizens. Engaging communities can unlock vital local knowledge, promote buy-in from the populace, and ensure that projects are responsive to societal requirements.

An approach to urban planning that takes into account the interests of local communities can help mitigate social inequality by ensuring everyone has access to quality public services and sustainable living conditions, regardless of their income level. Furthermore, it promotes economic sustainability by maximizing the match between people's skills and the opportunities available in the city.

The insights and creativity of local residents can even contribute to environmental sustainability. Residents often possess a keen understanding of local ecological systems and have local, inventive ideas for mitigating harmful impacts on the environment while improving urban infrastructures, service delivery, and overall quality of life.

10.2. Tools for Engaging Communities

There are numerous tools available to planners, technocrats, and developers for engaging communities in sustainable city development. These include community workshops, focus groups, public forums, social media engagement, and crowdsourcing platforms.

1. Community Workshops: These are targeted, interactive events where residents can share ideas and help plan aspects of sustainable development projects. Workshops can be organized around specific themes or regions within a city.

2. Focus Groups: These small-group discussions provide more in-depth insights into community needs, values, and perceptions. They are especially useful when dealing with complex topics that require detailed feedback.

3. Public Forums: Held in accessible, high-capacity venues, public forums allow for a broad range of community members to express their views and ask questions about upcoming projects.

4. Social Media Engagement: The ubiquity of social media has made it an essential tool for reaching out to communities, especially younger generations. Planners and developers can use these platforms to share information, ask for input, and respond to questions and concerns.

5. Crowdsourcing Platforms: Digital platforms enable communities to share their ideas and feedback in a structured, organized manner. They are particularly useful for ongoing engagement and collaboration.

10.3. The Role of Technology in Community Engagement

Technology can play a critical role in community engagement. It can bridge communication gaps and enable the introduction of participatory governance mechanisms.

Digital mapping tools, for instance, can visualize the potential impacts of various development scenarios, helping community members understand and provide constructive feedback. Mobile applications can make participation more accessible and convenient, while smart city data can be made open to the public, fostering transparency and trust, informing decision-making, and enabling residents to contribute to solutions to shared problems.

10.4. Local Government Support

While community engagement is essential, it also requires support and facilitation from local governments. Public authorities can set the framework for participation, creating an openness and willingness to accept and work with community inputs.

Cities should endeavor to establish clear, inclusive, and flexible frameworks for community engagement, ensuring that all portions of the community are given an opportunity to get involved. This includes disadvantaged groups, minorities, youth, and the elderly.

10.5. Engaging Communities through Education and Empowerment

One practical way for increasing community engagement is through education and empowerment. This can be accomplished by providing information sessions, running awareness campaigns, and offering training programs on sustainability practices.

Having informed and equipped citizens not only enhances the capacity of communities to engage decision-makers in sustainable city development, but it also creates a culture of environmental stewardship and sustainable living.

10.6. Challenges and How to Overcome Them

Community engagement, although deeply enriching and beneficial, is not without its challenges. These can stem from socio-cultural dynamics, lack of trust, and limited capacity.

Socio-cultural dynamics within communities require an understanding of cultural sensitivities and local customs. Overcoming this challenge can involve embedding engagement processes in familiar and trusted local structures and utilizing local facilitators.

Building trust can be a difficult but vital process in community engagement. Transparency, consistent communication, and inclusive and responsive actions are fundamental building blocks.

Limited capacity within communities can hinder effective engagement. Investing in capacity-building programs can improve community-led participation and strengthen local ownership of sustainable city development initiatives.

To conclude, whilst a path of challenges, community engagement is a journey worth undertaking. As our planet grows more urbanized, engaging communities in sustainable development becomes an increasingly critical ingredient in crafting our metropolises of the future.

Chapter 11. Forging Ahead: Strategic Policies for Future Smart Cities

Pioneering an age of smart cities is no easy task. Its intricacy lies in amalgamating sustainable development, technological innovation, and intelligent infrastructure, while ensuring the populace is at the heart of this transformation.

11.1. Develop and Implement Green Policies

We must tailor our policies, keeping in mind the objective: cities that are technically advanced, yet eco-friendly and sustainable. Policies should encourage greener buildings with emphasis on natural light, renewable energy resources, and efficient insulation. They should also incentivize businesses to reduce carbon footprints, meanwhile, encouraging individuals to discard the use of fossil fuels.

Active modes of transportation like cycling, walking and public transportation ought to be promoted to reduce vehicular emissions. Building bike lanes and ensuring walkability should therefore be the priority of developmental policies.

City planners and policymakers also need to promote urban agriculture and green spaces. This will not only offset carbon emissions but also provide recreational spots, ultimately contributing to the mental well-being of the residents.

11.2. Powering Cities with Renewable Energy Sources

Transitioning to renewable energy is the cornerstone of developing smart cities. Solar, wind, hydro and geothermal energy sources are not only sustainable but also reduce dependence on non-renewable sources.

Cities, with their buildings, bridges, and roads— can become giant solar fields. Photovoltaic panels installed on rooftops, solar path lights, and solar-powered public transportation can all harness sunlight for power.

Wind turbines can supplement this solar energy, offering another renewable energy source while hydropower, biomass, and geothermal energy can provide the rest of the required power.

11.3. Implementing Efficient Waste Management Systems

Waste management is inherently a problem in densely populated cities. Smart cities, however, will need to innovate and sustainably manage their waste.

Landfill diversion strategies can be operationalized, prioritizing recycling and composting. Waste-to-energy plants, which combust waste to generate electricity, is another strategic solution.

Smart sensors mounted on waste bins connected to an AI-powered Waste Management System can provide data on fill-levels and optimize collection schedules.

11.4. Incorporating Technology and Data Analysis

A smart city relies heavily on the strategic use of data and technology. Sensors and IoT devices can generate data which, upon analysis, can provide invaluable insights into reducing energy consumption, managing traffic, and predicting infrastructural stress.

City planners can apply artificial intelligence and Machine Learning techniques for analyzing data, ultimately shaping city management decisions more efficiently.

11.5. Citizen Participation and Training

Citizens are not only users but also the creators and maintainers of smart city systems, so their participation is imperative. Regular workshops, training sessions, and awareness drives can ensure that people understand the technology and systems around them and make the most of them.

11.6. Partnerships with Private Sector

Public-private partnerships can serve as a catalyst in realizing the vision of a smart city. Governments can leverage the innovative capability of private enterprises to design cutting-edge solutions, contributing to efficient urban planning and management.

11.7. Legal Frameworks and Data Privacy

As the digital landscape expands with the advent of smart cities, implementing a concrete legal framework to protect data privacy is essential. Resident feedback should be incorporated into these policies to ensure transparency and trust.

In conclusion, there needs to be a holistic, concerted effort to foster smart cities, linking technology with eco-friendly practices, and making sure the actions taken have the people's interests at heart. Decisions at every level - from policymaking to management - have to be smart to realize the dream of a sustainable, brighter, and smarter future. After all, if we don't plan for the future today, we might not have one tomorrow.

www.ingramcontent.com/pod-product-compliance
Lightning Source LLC
LaVergne TN
LVHW051626050326
832903LV00033B/4685